CompTIA Project+ Beginners Guide:
Exam PK0-004

Table of Contents

Introduction

Project management is an area which is gaining popularity in today's world. Every day, you see project management jobs being advertised. You may also have a project which you need to undertake for your own gain. This calls for you to posses the necessary project management skills. This book is a guide for you on how to manage projects. It guides you on the various aspects of project management from the time the project idea is conceptualized to the time the project is completed. The book is the best for those who need to pass the CompTIA Project+- Exam PK0-004 exam. Enjoy reading!

Chapter 1- Project Basics

Project Properties

1. Temporary- a project is a temporary endeavor, meaning that it has an end.

2. Definite Start and finish- a project is constrained by time, so it has a definite start and finish. The project has predecessors and dependencies, so it has to be done based on a schedule.

3. Unique- a project delivers a unique product, service, or results. The results of a project can be tangible or intangible.

4. Reason- a project should have a reason as to why it was started, and a purpose it is expected to accomplish.

5. Project as part of program- programs and projects usually go hand in hand. A handoff to operations usually occurs at the end of each project.

6. Project as part of a portfolio- a project can be used as a portfolio for the projects which have been completed.

Project roles and responsibilities
Sponsor/champion

This is the person who commissions others to deliver a project, and champions its cause throughout the project. He has the following responsibilities:

- Funding/Finances the project.
- Defining the project charter or the scope.
- Setting the initial or baseline standards.
- Setting the initial goals/ high-level requirements.
- Controlling the go and no-go decisions..
- Marketing the project to ensure that others see it.

- Overcoming roadblocks to the development of the project.
- Justification of the business case.
- Acts as the approval authority by signing off on the project.

Project Manager

This is the person responsible for definition and development of the project in conjunction with the project sponsor. He has to ensure that the project is delivered to the agreed quality standards, in time, and within the agreed upon budget. He has the following responsibilities:

- Managing the co-ordination of partners and working groups which are engaged in the project work.
- Developing and maintaining a well detailed project plan.
- Managing the project deliverables in conjunction with project plan.
- Recording and management of project issues and escalation where necessary.
- Resolving the cross-functional issues at the project level.
- Managing the project scope and change control and escalating issues where necessary.
- Monitoring the project progress as well as its performance.
- Providing the status reports to project sponsor.
- Managing the project training within a specified budget.
- Working too close with the users as a way of ensuring that their needs are met.
- Defining and managing the User Acceptance Testing program.
- Approving the design specification.
- Delivering reports to the IPSC board on a regular basis.

Project coordinator

He is responsible for coordinating the stakeholders and the activities of a project. He has the following roles:

- Support the project manager.
- Cross-functional coordination.
- Documentation/administrative support.
- Time and resource scheduling.
- Check for quality.

Stakeholder

This is a person who has expressed his interest in the project, and he has a direct or indirect influence on the project. He has the following roles:

- Vested interest.
- Providing input and requirements to the project.
- Project steering.
- Providing any necessary expertise.

Scheduler

This is the person setting the schedule for the project. He has the following roles:

- Develop and maintain schedule for the project.
- Communicate the timeline and changes to the necessary parties.
- Reporting the schedule performance.
- Soliciting the task status from resources.

Project Team

These are the people who are responsible for providing the necessary expertise so as to develop the project. They have the following roles:

- Contribute the necessary expertise to the project.
- Contribute the deliverables according to the schedule.
- Estimation of the task duration.
- Estimation of the costs and dependencies.

Project Management Office (PMO)

This is the body which is responsible for setting organization standards so as to ensure that projects are delivered in the required standard. It has the following roles:

- Setting standards and practices for the organization.
- Setting the deliverables.
- Providing governance.
- Setting the key performance indicators as well as the parameters.
- Providing the necessary tools for project development.
- Outlining the consequences of non-performance.
- Documenting standards and setting their templates.
- Coordinating the necessary resources between the projects.

The Standard Project Phases

The following are the standard phases of a project:

1. Initiation
   This is the phase in which the business case for the project is defined. The high-level scope of the project is also defined in this project. Each project has the associated risks. The high level risks for a project should be defined in this phase. The result of this phase is the "project charter."

2. Planning
   In the planning phase, the project schedule has to be established so as to know the right time to complete it.

Since there are several parties involved in the development of the project, a work breakdown structure has to be created, and each party is assigned their task. The resources which are necessary for development of the project are determined and assembled. A means by which the members of the development team will be communicating by is established. Changes may also occur in the late phases of the project. A plan on how to manage changes is also established. The result of this phase is a "requirements specification document."

3. Execution
   This is the phase in which the actual project is being developed. The results of this phase are the "deliverables" for the project. A working project is delivered in this phase.

4. Monitor and Control
   This is the phase in which the performance of the project is monitored, and the necessary adjustments are made. The project has to be monitored so that any risks which arise are dealt with in the right time. Any issues to do with performance have to be identified and reported, and the necessary action will be taken.

5. Closing
   Here, a complete project is presented. The contractors who had been hired so as to work on the project will be terminated in this phase. The valuable members of the team are recognized. All the project documents have to be archived in this stage.

Project Cost Control

1. Total project cost
   At the initial phases of planning, you have to determine the total cost of the project. The budget should then be

followed whenever you are making payments for the costs incurred during project life cycle. A lot of research and critical thinking is needed for you to determine the total cost for your project.

Also, it is good for you to be aware that the costs may not remain to be the same throughout the life cycle of the project. This calls for you to give room for adjustments. For you to get profit from a project, ensure that you stick within the project budget.

2. Expenditure tracking
It is also good for you to keep track of your project costs. The budget that you prepare has to be time-based. This will help you to keep track of the project budget in phases. The actual cost of the project will have to be estimated against periodic targets which have been specified in the budget. The targets can be set on a weekly, monthly, or even yearly basis, depending on the length of the project.

Dividing the project cost into phases is better, compared to estimating the entire cost of the whole project. If there is some new work which needs to be done, it will be good for you to determine its cost and check to see if it can be accommodated in your estimated budget.

3. Burn Rate
This helps us to determine the performance of a project in comparison to the initially agreed budget. It helps us know the rate at which a project is spending its original budget.

4. Cost baseline/budget
This is the phased plan which has been approved. Once the budget has been created and approved, the project manager has to publish the baseline, and this should be

used as the base for comparison with the actual performance of the project.

Project Team Organizational Structures
Functional

This is managed in the hierarchical organization structure of the organization. The components of the project are taken by functional units, and each unit will take the responsibility for each charged component.

This structure has an advantage in that the personnel used is of greater flexibility. Also, in case some members of the project team exit, then the functions will be used so as to ensure that there is continuity of the project. The disadvantage with this structure is that the projects lack focus, with each unit having its own core functions of the general business.

Project-based Organizational Structure

This is the process of creating an independent protect team, and the management of the team is separated from the organization's management.

The advantage with this type of organization is that the team is only left with development of the team, and there is no multiple leadership. Also, the time for reaction is short, as the team is responsible for making project decisions. Also, each individual clearly understands his responsibilities within the project team.

Matrix Organizational Structure

This type is organized in a matrix form. In a functional matrix, the functional managers are granted greater power than the project managers. In the "project matrix," the project managers are granted more powers compared to the functional managers. In a balance matrix, both the project managers and the functional managers are granted equal powers.

With this type of organization, it is possible for resources to be shared among multiple projects. Due to the manager who is focused only on the work, he will be more careful with the details of the project. If the company has multiple projects, then it will be possible for them to balance the available resources as a way of ensuring that each project is completed within the agreed upon time.

The problem with this type of organization is that sharing of the resources among the available projects may lead to conflicts. Also, with this type of organization, some tension rises between the project manager and the functional manager. Also, before the project can be implemented, the project manager has to negotiate and consult with the managers of the department, which leads to a long process and thereafter delay.

Execute and Develop Project Schedules
Scheduling activities

To schedule the project activities, just follow the steps given below:

1. Determine tasks- you should first determine the tasks which are involved in each activity. Once you have learned these tasks, you can move to the next step.

2. Determine task start/finish- this involves setting the baseline. Determine and establish the start and finish times for the project. Any resources which are needed should be identified and assigned accordingly. The baseline will help us compare the way the project is progressing to the baseline which had been initially set.

3. Determine activity/task durations- this should involve determining the actual time that each activity will take to be completed. This should be the time the activity is started to the time it is completed.

4. Determine milestones- milestones are the targets which if achieved will mark success. These will help you to steer the project in the right direction. You have to set these for your project.

5. Set predecessors- before a project is started, there must be some activities which must be done first. These are called the predecessors. Again, the activities for a project cannot all be done at once. One activity has to come before another, and yet another activity has to come after the next one. To show the sequence of activities in a diagram, you can use a network diagram or a Gantt chart.

6. Set dependencies- each project has dependencies. The dependencies or the relations between the activities of a project determine the order in which these tasks should

be accomplished. There are four types of project dependencies which include the following:

- Finish to Start- in this type, the predecessors has to be finished before the successors can begin.
- Start to Start- the predecessor has to start before the success can finish.
- Finish to Finish- predecessors must finish before the successors can be finished.
- Start to Finish- the predecessor must finish before the successor can finish.

With dependencies, we are able to define how the preceding and the succeeding tasks are related. The finish-to-start forms the most common type of dependency in the majority of projects.

7. Prioritize tasks- for a project to run successfully, the task which constitutes it must be prioritized. You should arrange them from the task with the highest priority to the one with the lowest priority.

8. Determine critical path- the critical path is formed by the activities in the project which if delayed, the completion of the entire project will be delayed. The best way to identify these is by creating a network diagram or a Gantt chart.

9. Allocate resources- each task or activity within the project needs some resources so as to get completed. The resources include economic resources, time, technical expertise, and others.

10. Set baseline- this should specify the standard of the project, and it should be adhered to so as to ensure that the project runs successfully.

11. Set quality gates- quality gates should help you ensure that the final project is delivered in its best quality.

Work Breakdown Structure

This is a hierarchical breakdown of the tasks which are needed for the product or service to be delivered. It helps the project manager to determine the time it will take to complete the project, and the resources which are necessary for the project to be completed, as well as the other resources which are needed.

The following are the necessary steps for you to develop a work breakdown structure:

1. Determine the strategy for developing the work breakdown structure
   Plan to meet the project development team, as well as the others who are capable of developing the WBS. Since the team is experienced in other projects, they will help in providing the necessary expertise so as to develop the WBS. Any new tasks or the tasks which had been forgotten will be remembered.

2. Determine the highest level components of work which are to be accomplished

   The first level components for grouping work logically include the following:

   - Product deliverables- such as the project plan and the project charter.
   - Life Cycle phases- such as Analyze, Design, and Build.
   - Functions- such as Create New Employee, Update Salary, etc.
   - Organizational responsibility- such as Network Services and Finance.

3. Break the work process into small components
   Your aim in this case should be to break down each high level process into small components which are detailed enough for an accurate estimation of both time and other resources such as finances. The WBS should be broken down into the level of detail you are able to understand. For projects which are to span a long period of time, this might be challenging to you. This will make it easy for you to understand when reading it, and the overall work will be specified.

4. Name the component
   The name of the component should actually describe the kind of work which is to be done. Make sure that you use the noun-verb format, as it will make it easy for you to understand each component. Examples of component names include the following:

   - Document User Manual

   - Install Network Routers

   - Review Project Charter

5. Ensure that the work has been broken down to the lowest level that you desire
   There are various ways that you can ensure that you reach this. Assign each staff resource to only a single task. However, this is general; there are some circumstances under which you will have to assign a team to a single task. Two people may also have to work side by side so as to deliver the final product from the task. Each task should have results which are clearly identified.

   Also, ensure that a reasonable amount of time is taken so as to accomplish each individual task. It is highly recommended that you complete each work task within a period of two weeks, or even less than this if possible. The task has to convey the work which is to be accomplished. Each task has to be at the level at which you are capable of assigning costs. This calls for you to be careful when doing the work breakdown. The task should be small enough so that it would be easy for you to assign a reasonable amount of time.

Aspects of the Agile Methodology

Agile is a project development methodology which provides an alternative to the traditional waterfall project development method. It is based on delivering the project within short cycles of small increments. The following are some of the aspects of the agile methodology:

Readily adapt to changing/new requirements

The agile method is capable of adapting or accepting changes to the project, even in the late stages of development, and the previous versions of the project will remain unchanged.

This is not the case with the other project development methodologies. This makes agile the best project development methodology in cases where the project requirements are not clear at the initial stages or they are dynamic, in that they are expected to change in the future.

Iterative approach

In agile, the project or the product is released in small deliverables after a short development cycle, usually known as «iteration." The product from each iteration has to be tested in the presence of the users. Once the users accept, the development team has to move on into the next iteration.

Note that the team cannot move into the next iteration before the current one is accepted. After each iteration, the next iteration aims at delivering a product whose quality is higher than the one of the previous deliverable.

Continuous requirements gathering

In agile, the development has to keep on gathering the project requirements from the necessary sources continuously. The best time to do this is after a certain deliverable has been delivered to the users and before beginning the next iteration. During the testing of each deliverable, users should be asked what they expect from the next deliverable. This is a good way of ensuring that the needs of the users are met to their satisfaction.

Establish a backlog

This should have a list of the features or the technical tasks which the team will maintain and help them to create each release. If there is an item in the backlog which is not contributing in any way to the success of the project, it should be removed. With the backlog, it will be easy for the team to set expectations together with the stakeholders of the project.

The most important items for the project should be written first in the backlog, and end with the less pressing requirements. This will help the team do each task at the right time during the project duration.

Burn down charts

This is a graphical representation which can help you to track the progress of your project. The chart shows a graphical relationship between the efforts put in the project against the work which has been delivered.

Before this chart can be created, the total work has to be broken down. Each activity in the project then has to be assigned a number of hours by which it should be accomplished. It is after this that the burn down chart can be plotted.

Continuous feedback

In agile, each iteration results in a product which is deliverable to the users. The product is then tested in the presence of users, who will accept or reject the product. The users are able to give their feedback in terms of the quality of the product. This is done at the end of each iteration, meaning that the development team will be able to get continuous feedback from the users. With this, it will be hard for the team to veer off from the main goal of creating the project.

Sprint planning

This involves calling for a sprint meeting so as to plan and come to an agreement regarding the plans which have been written in the backlog. A sprint session should be held only once, and should not take more than one hour.

During this meeting, the team has to agree on the backlog items which they will accomplish. Don't spend more than an hour in the sprint meeting, as you may spend too much time in unnecessary planning.

Daily standup meetings/SCRUM meetings

During sprint, the team has to hold daily sprint meetings, usually known as the "daily scrum." These meetings are normally held at the same time each day and at the same venue.

In most cases, the scrum meetings are held in the morning so as to plan the context of the next day. To ensure that the meeting is relevant, a small amount of time is spent in the meeting.

SCRUM Retrospective

This is a meeting in agile project development at the end of each iteration. It is during this meeting that the team will determine what has happened during the meeting and then look for areas of improvement in the next iterations.

During this meeting, each member of the team has to answer the questions given below:

- What worked well?

- What failed to work well for us?

- What actions can be taken to improve the process going forward?

This meeting can be seen as a way of identifying the lessons which were learned and how to do the necessary improvements.

They have to decide what has been happening and the actions which should be taken as a way of enhancing the efficiency of the next iterations. The important point to be arrived at in these meetings is the best ways to make improvements.

Self-organized and Self-directed teams

Agile teams are self-directed, which means that after they have been assigned a task to accomplish, they are tasked with the responsibility of sorting out any challenges they face. This is actually what happens in the agile methodology. The development team has to sort out the challenges they face in a bid to deliver the product in time, desired quality, and to satisfy the users. The team is also self-organized, as they have to assign tasks to each member appropriately.

Human Resource, Physical Resource, and Personnel Management
Resource management concepts

1. Resource over allocation
    This happens when more tasks are assigned than what a particular resource is capable of handling. This is a common occurrence in companies with more projects and small resources.

2. Shared resources
    This occurs when a particular resource is used for more than one project or shared resources are used in more than one project, in which all the resource information may be assigned to a single file named a "resource pool."

3. Dedicated resources
    This is a resource which is assigned to a single project alone as opposed to a shared resource which may be assigned to more projects.

4. Resource allocation
    This involves allocation as well as scheduling of the resources which are available in an effective and economical manner.

5. Resource shortage
    This refers to the unavailability of enough resources to handle the projects which are being undertaken in a company. It is a common occurrence in companies which run too many projects.

6. Low quality resources
    The quality of resources determines the success or the quality of the final product. Resources with a good quality will enhance the delivery of high quality products, while resources of low quality will lead to the delivery of low quality products. The use of low quality resources in

project development may lead to user dissatisfaction, and hence failure of the project.

7. Interproject dependencies
These help you show that a certain project is dependent on the completion of the deliverables of the other projects so that it can be successful. Once you have established the interproject dependencies, you will be able to document and track the projects without having to cause scheduling shifts.

Personnel Management

This refers to the process of getting and then maintaining a satisfied and satisfactory workforce. Whenever people are assembled into a team to work on a similar project towards achieving a common goal, there is a need to manage them to ensure that the objectives are attained.

The following are the various aspects of personnel management in project management:

1. Team Building- this refers to any activity which is carried out as a way of improving interpersonal relations and increases the cohesiveness of the team.

2. Trust building- trust is very essential for a project to run successfully. Without trust, the project team will find themselves battling constantly, which will result in a failed project. The project manager is always held accountable for the culture of the project team, so he has to look for ways to build trust among the project team members.

3. Team selection- the process of choosing people to complete a certain project is very critical. This is because these people will be working towards achieving a similar goal. The project manager should do it

carefully to ensure the project runs smoothly. You have to choose a mix of skills to ensure each task is completed successfully.

4. Conflict resolution- conflicts must occur during project development, and these must be resoolved for a smooth running environment. In forcing one party out so as to win its own position, and ignores the concerns and needs of the other party. One party wins, while the other party loses. In smoothing, the emphasis is on the areas which have been agreed, but the disagreed areas are downplayed.

Chapter 2- Project Constraints

In project management, a constraint is any restriction which defines the limitations of the project. The following are the common constraints for projects:

1. Time- this is the actual time which is needed for a deliverable to be delivered, which is the end result of the project. This is determined by the amount of time required and the amount of resources allocated to the project.

2. Cost- this is the estimated amount of money needed to complete a project. It includes the resources, bills for materials, risk estimates, labor rates for the contractors, etc.

3. Scope- these refer to the functional requirements for a project which, if completed, will form a deliverable. The success of the scope is determined by the quality of the delivered product.

4. Quality- this refers to how correct and successful the delivered product is. If the goal of the project is achieved, the quality of the project will be considered to be high.

5. Risk- these are the uncertainties, or the threats to the project. Of course, there are many risks which face any particular project, and these usually vary from project to project.

6. Resources- these include budget, people, and assets which are required for people to deliver the project.

Risk Strategies and Activities

The following are the risk assessment strategies:

1. Mitigate risk- these are the activities which are more likely to occur, but they have a small financial impact. The best approach to respond to this is by using the management control systems for the purpose of reducing the risk of the potential loss.

2. Avoid risk- this is for the activities whose likelihood of occurring is high, but they have a small financial impact. To respond to this, just avoid the activity.

3. Transfer risk- these are the activities whose probability of occurring is low, but they have a large financial impact. The best way for one to respond to this is by transferring the whole or part of the risk to a third party by purchasing an insurance cover, outsourcing, hedging, or joining partnerships.

4. Accept risks- if cost-benefit analysis finds the cost for mitigating risk is higher than the cost for bearing the risk, the best response is accepting and continuously monitoring the risk.

Chapter 3- Communication and Change Management

The following are some of the communication methods in project management:

1. Email- the emails should be used for sending routine messages, sharing information, and sending messages which are related to marketing. These should be spread out so that the emails are not sent to the same people over a short period of time.

2. Meetings- the project manager may choose to organize schedule meetings, impromptu meetings, kick off meetings, or closure meetings.

3. Voice conferencing- this can help organize for meetings using only voice, even if those who are expected to participate are in different geographical locations.

Other forms of communication which can be used include instant messaging, face-to-face, text message, or social media, as well as the distribution of the printed media.

Factors Influencing Communication

1. Language barriers- the parties must use a language which each one understands. The people participating in a project come from different backgrounds, so a common language should be used.

2. Cultural differences- the cultural differences inside and outside an organization influence the choice of a communication method.

3. Personal differences- this includes the personality of the receiver, his traits, and age, as well as the style they prefer.

4. Time zones/geographical factors- the people participating in a communication process might be located in different regions. Different regions in the world are in different time zones, explaining the differences in time throughout the world. This affects the choice of communication method.

5. Rapport building/Relationship building- during the process of project development, the project manager may need to build a good relationship among those participating in the project. This greatly influences the choice of communication method.

6. Stakeholder requirement- the needs of the stakeholders influence the communication method which is to be used. The stakeholders may need frequent communication which makes them use a certain method of communication. The level of confidentiality which is needed by the stakeholders will also influence the choice of communication method. The level of report detail also influences this.

Communication Triggers

The following are some of the triggers to communication in project management:

1. Audits- the need to pass auditing information to the stakeholders may cause the need for communication. This can be on a regular or periodic basis. The stakeholder, the project manager, and the sponsor may be involved in this communication.

2. Project planning- the need to identify challenges and plan for them before they occur. The project manager and the project champion are involved.

3. Project change- the audience in this can include the project manager, the sponsor, and the stakeholders. The communication can happen anytime during the execution of the project. The aim is to keep the project's constraints according to what was agreed.

4. Risk register updates- the audience for this communication includes the project manager, project scheduler, and project coordinator. It happens during the planning and execution phases. The risks are quantified so that appropriate actions may be taken.

5. Milestones- the audience for this communication includes the project manager, project sponsor, project scheduler, stakeholders and project coordinator. The communication can be done at any time. The aim is to know where, when, and how much the schedule change impacts the project schedule.

6. Task initiation/completion
The audience in this case will include the team members, project manager, stakeholders, and project scheduler. It helps to determine and set when tasks can begin and then the necessary resources for these tasks to complete are coordinated.

7. Stakeholder changes
The audience in this case includes the project manager, project sponsor, stakeholders, and some project teams. The communication can be done during the project phases. The teams which have been affected by the change have to be communicated to.

8. Gate reviews
The audience in this case may include the project manager, project sponsor and stakeholders. This communication should be done at a specific point of the project development so as to make a go or a no go

decision. This is the decision which is to be reached during this communication.

9. Business continuity response
The audience in this case includes the new project sponsor, the new project manager and the stakeholders. This communication has to be done whenever there are changes in the management. The goal of doing this communication is to show that the leadership is helping and directing this transition.

10. Incident response
The audience targeted during this communication includes the project manager, project sponsor and the champion stakeholders. It has to be done whenever an incidence which can change the direction of the project has occurred. It is a way of showing that the leadership is complying with the initial agreement.

11. Resource changes
The audience in this case includes the project managers, the stakeholders, the project sponsor, and the project teams. This communication can be done at anytime during the project development. The teams which have been affected by the change have to be addressed directly during this communication. This will help them know more about the changes.

Organizational change

These include the following:

1. Business merger/acquisition- this type of change is good for cultural integration and any efforts related to change. The potential areas of conflict should be assessed, and their strengths and weaknesses determined. A comprehensive communication plan is also necessary. The business disruptions should be reduced, but its readiness increased.

2. Business demerger/split
   Make sure you understand the process, the system, and the procedure used and the compliances. The cost of the risk should thoroughly be evaluated. Develop workarounds and simulate the demerger processes. The simulated model should then be implemented for change.

3. Business process change- this includes technological developments, new innovations, and implementation of information systems.

4. International organization- This can also be referred to as the strategic change. It helps an organization to increase its benefits and cut down any unintended consequences. The work and workflow within the organization are organized for accomplishment of purposes. This type of organization is also done to enhance scalability and avoid complications. It leads to improved performance and efficiency.

5. Relocation- this change is objective oriented. It allows for a 2-way communication. Active listening is practiced as a way of listening and accepting the ideas received from all levels of the organization. The small victories which are achieved motivate the achievement of the bigger ones. The aim of this change is to assign the right jobs to the right people.

6. Outsourcing- there is a tailored communication for every stakeholder group. A transition strategy is necessary, which includes the redeployment of the resources, severance, work, and retention policies. A design strategy is needed for the leadership changes or the leadership integration. Change acceptance strategies are also needed. Training has to be done so as to help the team members know how to work and interact with the provider.

Project Changes

The following are some of the changes which can be implemented or done on a project:

1. Timeline change- this is the change in the schedule of the project. This can be a change in the time that a particular activity will start or end, or a change in the time during which the project will end.

2. Funding change- the budget allocated to a project may change. This might be as a result of the need for additional resources or an increase in the length of the entire project.

3. Requirements change- the initial requirements for a project may change with time. This is because of the dynamic nature of the environment we live in. Also, most user requirements are not clear in the early phases of a project. Due to this, they may find a new discovery as the project is being developed, and this will call for a change in the project requirements.

4. Quality change- of course, the project is expected to be delivered at a certain quality. This means that it has met some quality standards. However, such requirements may also change.

5. Resource- this involves a change in the resources which are being used for the project development.

6. Scope change- each project is expected to cover a number of areas, or have a number of features after completion. However, new features may be added to the project or some may be excluded from the project.

Chapter 4- Project Tools and Documentation

Project Management Tools

This is software which can help you track the schedule of your product. There are many software programs which can help you do this. During project planning, it may be hard for you to choose the best software for your use.

The ability for the software to display a Network diagram and a Gantt chart should be a must. Also, the price of the software should be considered as some of them will come at a higher price than the budget for your entire project. You should know how familiar the project team is in terms of using the software.

Some of the common project management software tools include Microsoft Project, ZOHO projects, FastTrack Schedule 9, Workfront, and others.

Charts

Charts are good tools for project management. There are different kinds of charts which can be used for project management, and the aim of all these charts is to help you visualize your project.

The Gantt chart helps you to schedule your project. Gantt charts are good for showing the project dependencies, the start and stop times for project tasks, and it provides a frame which can help anyone in the project for visualization. It helps one to easily calculate the critical path. Gantt charts are only good for small projects.

In the case of more complex projects, one can use the PERT chart, commonly known as the network diagram. This can be used for projects which are complex and it will show the relationships between the project activities. Rather than visualizing the whole of the project, it can help you to visualize part of it.

A histogram is also another chart which is popular in project management. It works well to help the project team improve the quality of their work by relying on historical data. You then have to choose the processes which you will improve. It can help you know where a problem which occurs more frequently is coming from.

Dashboard/status report

Communication between the teams which are involved in development of the project is very essential. There should be effective communication among the member of the project team, the sponsor, and the stakeholders. A project status report or dashboard is an effective and efficient way for you to express the status of your project at any time. There are a number of software programs which can allow you to create this report. A good example of this is Microsoft Excel.

Performance measurement tools

A project has objectives. A project should be completed in the planned budget, within the agreed upon time, and utilize the resources which had been planned for. A project is said to be successful if it accomplishes these.

It is always important for you to identify the KPIs (Key Performance Indicators) for your project, as these will help you know whether or not your project was successful. With this, the work of assessing the performance of your project will be easy.

The key indicators should be the items which if they are monitored properly, can help us assess the performance of the project. With the KPIs, it will be possible not only to see the performance of your project, but to predict any future problems with the project. This is good as you will handle this before a disaster impacts the project.

SWOT analysis

SWOT stands for Strengths, Weaknesses, Opportunities, and Threats. It represents the project areas which one can maximize so that the whole of the project can benefit. With this tool, the various aspects of the project can be evaluated, and then their potential maximized for the benefit of the entire project. If risks are identified, then the most effective ways for mitigating such risks are applied.

SWOT analysis is normally in the early phases of a project so that the project plan can be formed by the elements of this analysis. You can also use it in the later stages of the project in case you experience difficulties with scheduling, budget or deliverables and you need to bring your project back on track.

The strengths for the company include the budget, skills, business benefits once the project is completed, and experience. Competition in the market should be considered as a threat to the project, and this needs a lot of care when handling. During SWOT analysis, there are number of questions which you have to ask yourself. You then dive deeper into looking for solutions to these problems and this will help you understand the performance of your project.

Responsible, Accountable, Consulted, Informed (RACI) Matrix

It is always good for the project manager to delegate duties of the project as early as possible. The RACI model can help you accomplish this. Many people are involved in an individual project, and this calls for you to look for a way to avoid a situation in which the participators are competing so as to accomplish a particular task.

With the RACI model, you are able to easily identify the roles and responsibilities and then avoid confusion about those responsibilities. It includes the following:

1.   Responsibilities- this is the person responsible for doing some work so that a task can be accomplished. They are responsible for decision-making and doing the necessary work.

2.   Accountable- this is the person who is accountable for a through and correct completion of a task. He has to be one person, either the project sponsor or supervisor.

3.   Consulted- this is the person responsible for providing the project information as well as two-way communication. It involves several persons, mostly the subject matter experts.

4.   Informed- these refer to the people who must be constantly updated regarding the progress of the project and there is one-way communication. They are the people who are directly affected by the tasks.

Vendor-Centric or Partner documents

1. Request for Information – each project needs a supply of materials from the necessary supplier. This document helps you in choosing the right supply for the products. It helps you describe your procurement requirements and then release it to the market. The suppliers will then be required to register that they are interested in supplying the products.

2. Statement of work- this is a document which specifies the goods and the services which should be obtained from a supplier.

3. Request for Proposal- this is a document which states that the company has the necessary funds for completion of a project and that companies should begin to place their proposal for completing the project. It should clearly outline the bidding process, the terms and conditions for the contract, and how to format and then present the bid.

4. Request for Quote- this is a document which solicits the price and the delivery quotations which meet the minimum quality specifications for some specific quantity of goods and services. These are not advertised to the public. Companies usually send several of these so that they can an opportunity of comparing the bids from the various suppliers.

5. Mutually binding documents
   These are the documents which specify what has been agreed between a numbers of parties. It specifies a binding contact between parties, two or more, and it can be used for contingency purposes.

   A Non-Disclosure agreement is a document which outlines some confidential material, information, or parties, and this is usually between two or more parties which need to share information with each other. No party is allowed to disclose any information contained in the document. A letter of intent is simply a letter which shows the intention of the writer writing the letter.

A warranty is simply a guarantee by a manufacturer of a product about its quality and that the manufacturer will take responsibility in case a repair of the product is needed before the expiration of a certain period of time. A purchase order is a commercial document and the first official offer which is issued by the buyer to a seller and it indicates the types, the quantities, and the prices for the agreed goods and services. It is used when there is a need for control of the goods from any external supplier.

A Memorandum of Understanding specifies a formal agreement between two or more parties. Although these are not legally binding, they are a show of seriousness. A service agreement is simply a contract between a service provider and an end user defining the level of services which the service provider will provide to the end user. The main purpose of this document is just to specify the level of service which the user should expect to receive from the provider.

Conclusion

We have come to the end of this guide. The Project+ PK0-004 exam covers 4 topics. These topics are all about project management and its essentials. The exam tests on all topics regarding project management. Projects can be of various types, including software projects, construction and building projects, etc. This exam tackles these in general, so there is no focus on a particular type of project. It is a good exam for those who want to work as project managers, or for those who need to gain skills in project management. For you to pass the exam, you must understand all the phases of project development and what entails in these phases, right from the start to the completion of the project!

www.ingramcontent.com/pod-product-compliance
Lightning Source LLC
Chambersburg PA
CBHW070904070326
40690CB00009B/1992